DATE DUE

2 / 02

GAYLORD			PRINTED IN U.S.A.

SandCastle 2

Homophones

The Prince Left His Prints

Amanda Rondeau

Publishing Company

JACKSON COUNTY LIBRARY SERVICES
MEDFORD, OREGON 97501

Published by SandCastle™, an imprint of ABDO Publishing Company, 4940 Viking Drive, Edina, Minnesota 55435.

Cover and interior photo credits: Digital Stock, Digital Vision, Eyewire Images, PhotoDisc, Rubberball Productions

Library of Congress Cataloging-in-Publication Data

Rondeau, Amanda, 1974-
  The prince left his prints / Amanda Rondeau.
    p. cm. -- (Homophones)
  Includes index.
  Summary: Photographs and simple text present homonyms, words that sound the same but have different meanings.
  ISBN 1-57765-781-0
  1. English language--Homonyms--Juvenile literature. [1. English language--Homonyms.]
I. Title. II. Series.

PE1595 .R69 2002
428.1--dc21
                                                                          2001053403

The SandCastle concept, content, and reading method have been reviewed and approved by a national advisory board including literacy specialists, librarians, elementary school teachers, early childhood education professionals, and parents.

Let Us Know

After reading the book, SandCastle would like you to tell us your stories about reading. What is your favorite page? Was there something hard that you needed help with? Share the ups and downs of learning to read. We want to hear from you! To get posted on the ABDO Publishing Company Web site, send us email at:

sandcastle@abdopub.com

About SandCastle™
Nonfiction books for the beginning reader

- Basic concepts of phonics are incorporated with integrated language methods of reading instruction. Most words are short, and phrases, letter sounds, and word sounds are repeated.

- Book levels are based on the ATOS™ for Books formula. Other considerations for readability include the number of words in each sentence, the number of characters in each word, and word lists based on curriculum frameworks.

- Full-color photography reinforces word meanings and concepts.

- "Words I Can Read" list at the end of each book teaches basic elements of grammar, helps the reader recognize the words in the text, and builds vocabulary.

- Reading levels are indicated by the number of flags on the castle.

SandCastle uses the following definitions for this series:

- Homographs: words that are spelled the same but sound different and have different meanings. *Easy memory tip: "-graph"= same look*

- Homonyms: words that are spelled and sound the same but have different meanings. *Easy memory tip: "-nym"= same name*

- Homophones: words that sound alike but are spelled differently and have different meanings. *Easy memory tip: "-phone"= sound alike*

Look for more SandCastle books in these three reading levels:

Level 1	**Level 2**	**Level 3**
(one flag)	(two flags)	(three flags)

Grades Pre-K to K	**Grades K to 1**	**Grades 1 to 2**
5 or fewer words per page	5 to 10 words per page	10 to 15 words per page

Note: Some pages in this book contain more than 10 words in order to more clearly convey the concept of the book.

plain

plane

Homophones are words that sound alike but are spelled differently and have different meanings.

Mai is wearing a pale yellow shirt.

The baby has a green pail.

Molly hurt her ankle and feels pain.

James is careful not to paint the glass pane.

I feel at peace when my dad holds me.

I ate a piece of watermelon.

Wally peeks around the corner.

Some mountains have snow on their peaks.

Alex brings his fishing pole
to the river.

We took a poll in class.

Heidi prays before going to bed.

My art project received praise.

Lee pried off the wood.

We show our national pride
by waving the flag.

Poor kitty.

She wants to get the fish.

What did Jason pour on his mom?

(water)

Words I Can Read

Nouns

A noun is a person, place, or thing

ankle (ANG-kuhl) p. 8

art (ART) p. 17

baby (BAY-bee) p. 7

bed (BED) p. 16

class (KLASS) p. 15

corner (KOR-nur) p. 12

dad (DAD) p. 10

fish (FISH) p. 20

fishing (FISH-ing) p. 14

flag (FLAG) p. 19

kitty (KIT-ee) p. 20

mom (MOM) p. 21

pail (PAYL) p. 7

pain (PAYN) p. 8

pane (PAYN) p. 9

peace (PEESS) p. 10

piece (PEESS) p. 11

plain (PLANE) p. 4

plane (PLANE) p. 4

pole (POHL) p. 14

poll (POHL) p. 15

praise (PRAZE) p. 17

pride (PRIDE) p. 19

project (PROJ-ekt) p. 17

river (RIV-ur) p. 14

shirt (SHURT) p. 6

snow (SNOH) p. 13

water (WAW-tur) p. 21

watermelon (WAW-tur-mel-uhn) p. 11

wood (WUD) p. 18

Plural Nouns

A plural noun is more than one person, place, or thing

homophones (HOME-uh-fonez) p. 5

meanings (MEE-ningz) p. 5

mountains (MOUN-tuhnz) p. 13

peaks (PEEKSS) p. 13

words (WURDZ) p. 5

Proper Nouns
A proper noun is the name of a person, place, or thing

Alex (AL-ekss) p. 14
Heidi (HYE-dee) p. 16
James (JAYMZ) p. 9

Jason (JAYSS-uhn)
p. 21
Lee (LEE) p. 18

Mai (MYE) p. 6
Molly (MAHL-ee) p. 8
Wally (WAWL-ee)
p. 12

Verbs
A verb is an action or being word

are (AR) p. 5
ate (AYT) p. 11
brings (BRINGZ)
p. 14
did (DID) p. 21
feel (FEEL) p. 10
feels (FEELZ) p. 8
get (GET) p. 20
going (GOH-ing)
p. 16
has (HAZ) p. 7

have (HAV) pp. 5, 13
holds (HOHLDZ) p. 10
hurt (HURT) p. 8
is (IZ) pp. 6, 9
paint (PAYNT) p. 9
peeks (PEEKSS) p. 12
pour (POR) p. 21
prays (PRAYZ) p. 16
pried (PRIDE) p. 18
received (ri-SEEVD)
p. 17

show (SHOH) p. 19
sound (SOUND) p. 5
spelled (SPELD) p. 5
took (TUK) p. 15
wants (WONTSS)
p. 20
waving (WAYV-ing)
p. 19
wearing (WAIR-ing)
p. 6

Adjectives
An adjective describes something

alike (uh-LIKE) p. 5
careful (KAIR-fuhl)
p. 9
different
(DIF-ur-uhnt) p. 5
glass (GLASS) p. 9

green (GREEN) p. 7
her (HUR) p. 8
his (HIZ) pp. 14, 21
my (MYE) pp. 10, 17
national (NASH-
uh-nuhl) p. 19

our (OUR) p. 19
pale (PAYL) p. 6
poor (POR) p. 20
some (SUHM) p. 13
their (THAIR) p. 13
yellow (YEL-oh) p. 6

Match these homophones to the pictures

pain
pane

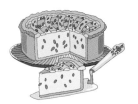

peace
piece

peaks
peeks

pole
poll